Title: The Thinking Dollar

Subtitle: How AI is Changing the Way We Use, Move, and Grow Money.

Author's Name: Raijo Nirmal

Table of Contents

To my sister and best friend,

Introduction

The Thinking Dollar: How AI is Changing the Way We Use, Move, and Grow Money

Not long ago, money was simple. You earned it, you saved it, you spent it. Maybe you tucked it away in a savings account, wrote a check, swiped a card. You checked your bank balance on payday and hoped it aligned with your mental math. That was finance — familiar, tactile, and largely human.

But those days are disappearing. Quickly.

Money, as we knew it, is being reimagined. It's no longer just paper in your wallet or digits in your bank app. Today, money is becoming intelligent — not because it thinks for itself, but because the systems around it do. Artificial intelligence, once confined to sci-fi movies and research labs, is now hardwired into how we earn, save, invest, borrow, and transact. We are entering a world where your financial advisor might be an algorithm, your mortgage underwriter a machine learning model, and your bank a set of code running in the cloud.

This book is about that transformation.

A Tectonic Shift in Finance

Artificial intelligence is not merely a new tool in the financial world it's a tectonic force reshaping its foundation. The financial sector, long known for its caution and conservatism, is now embracing something radically new: decision-making at the speed of light, based not on instinct or experience, but on pattern recognition, behavioral data, and predictive algorithms.

We see it everywhere. Robo-advisors are managing millions in client portfolios with zero human intervention. AI models are scanning thousands of economic signals to execute trades in milliseconds. Insurance claims are being processed in seconds by intelligent systems that never sleep. Even central banks are experimenting with AI to simulate monetary policy outcomes in real-time.

This shift is not hypothetical it's here. It's happening beneath our fingertips every time we tap to pay, apply for a loan, or invest a few dollars in an app. It's happening inside the very institutions that once required a handshake and a signature to move money.

Why I Wrote This Book

When I first started working in finance, the conversation was still human-centered. Advisors talked to clients. Bankers made judgment calls. Analysts built models in Excel. But even then, I sensed the change coming. Over the years, I've sat across boardrooms and bank desks, at start-up demo days and regulatory panels, watching finance evolve.

My fascination with both finance and technology has been lifelong—but it wasn't until I saw firsthand how AI systems were being deployed in areas like risk modeling, personal finance, and fraud detection that I realized we were in the middle of something far bigger than a digital upgrade. We were watching a new form of money emerge one that learns, adapts, and thinks. Thus, *The Thinking Dollar* was born.

I wrote this book for a wide audience:

- For the finance professional trying to stay ahead of the curve.
- For the student curious about the intersection of AI and economics.
- For the entrepreneur building the next FinTech product.

- And for the everyday person wondering what's happening to their bank, their wallet, their investments and their future.

This book aims to be your field guide to a rapidly shifting financial frontier.

What You Can Expect

In the chapters ahead, you'll explore how AI is not just a feature in finance - it's fast becoming the framework. We'll look at:

- **The rise of digital finance**: From biometric payments to smart contracts and crypto-powered wallets.
- **Intelligent investing**: How robo-advisors, predictive models, and AI-driven hedge funds are redefining wealth building.

- **The automation of credit**: How algorithms decide who gets a loan, and what biases and breakthroughs exist in that system.
- **The ethical crossroads**: What happens when machines decide your financial fate? Who's responsible when an AI makes a mistake?
- **The future of jobs and institutions**: Will AI replace bankers? Or empower them?

You'll hear real-world stories - some of staggering success, others cautionary. We'll dig into the mechanics of how AI works (in plain English), examine the people building these tools, and consider the policymakers trying to keep up.

And throughout, we'll come back to one simple idea: **Money is no longer just a number - it's a narrative built by data and told by machines.**

Why It Matters

This isn't just about technology. This is about trust. For centuries, we've trusted banks, regulators, accountants, advisors. Increasingly, we are transferring that trust to code. But how much do we really understand about the systems we now rely on? When AI becomes the gatekeeper to your mortgage, the brain behind your retirement portfolio, or the watchdog for your transactions, the implications ripple far beyond finance.

You don't need to be a data scientist to care about this. If you earn, spend, save, borrow, investor plan to you're already a participant in this new ecosystem. And in a world of invisible algorithms and black-box decision-making, understanding even the basics of AI's role in finance can be a form of empowerment.

A Personal Note

Over the years, I've had the chance to work across different corners of the financial world from legacy institutions to FinTech start-ups, from risk modeling to investment research. I've seen spreadsheets give way to smart models. I've seen slow-moving banks be outpaced by nimble AI-powered platforms. And I've also seen how easily we can forget that behind every technological shift, there are people affected by its outcomes.

That's why this book is written in plain language, not technical jargon. I want to invite you into the conversation not as a passive observer, but as a thinker, a builder, a questioner. The financial system is changing. This is your chance to understand how and why and to decide what role you'll play.

Welcome to *The Thinking Dollar*. A world where money no longer just moves, it learns.

Chapter 1: The AI Revolution in Finance

An intelligent revolution has silently started its quick transformation of the financial industry. Modern financial operations are currently undergoing transformative changes because of artificial intelligence which affects money transactions and organizational choices and trust-based business conduct worldwide. Artificial intelligence (AI) operates as the driver of this revolution to build a new financial system base. Science fiction and academic research previously classified AI but its evolutionary progress led to practical usage which generated profits that modernized banking and lending as well as transformed investing and insurance processes. This section shows how artificial intelligence progressed from financial tech external boundaries into its core systems while exploring the explosive speed at which it is transforming financial operations.

AI's Role in FinTech: From Niche to Necessity

At its heart, FinTech short for financial technology is about using modern tools to improve and innovate financial services. AI is no longer just one of those tools; it's the most transformative one of them all.

AI in FinTech includes technologies like:

- **Machine Learning (ML):** Systems that improve from experience without being explicitly programmed.

- **Natural Language Processing (NLP):** Enables machines to understand and communicate with humans in everyday language.
- **Computer Vision and Pattern Recognition:** For document verification and fraud detection.
- **Predictive Analytics:** Helping businesses and consumers forecast outcomes, such as credit risk or investment returns.

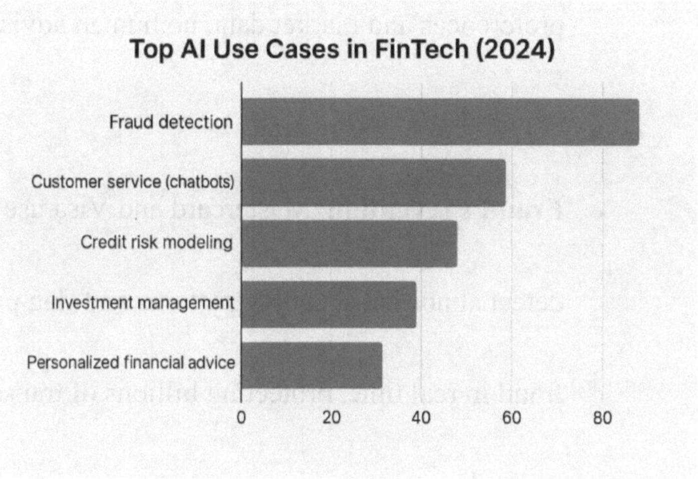

Let's look at some **real-life applications**:

- **Chatbots & Virtual Assistants**: AI-powered assistants like Erica (Bank of America) or Eno (Capital One) help millions of users manage transactions, set up alerts, and answer questions 24/7.
- **Robo-Advisors**: Platforms like Betterment and Wealthfront automate investing based on user preferences and market data, no human advisor required.
- **Fraud Prevention**: Mastercard and Visa use AI to detect abnormal spending patterns and flag potential fraud in real time, protecting billions of transactions every day.

- **Credit Risk Analysis**: Companies like Upstart use AI to assess borrower risk beyond credit scores, using alternative data points like education and employment history.

These are no longer experimental features – they are standard offerings in modern financial services. AI has become a non-negotiable competitive advantage.

Why AI Is Reshaping the Financial Industry

Traditional finance operated on three things: trust, time, and regulation. AI has fundamentally altered how those three pillars function.

1. Real-Time Decision Making

AI functions best in systems requiring immediate conclusion making capabilities. AI uses milliseconds to analyze more than one thousand data points from transaction records and GPS positions together with social behaviors to make immediate decisions:

- Loan approvals
- Fraud detection
- Credit card alerts
- Investment trades

This real-time capability is especially valuable in global markets where delays can cost millions—or even billions—of dollars.

2. Enhanced Security and Fraud Detection

Security is the backbone of finance. AI enhances this by detecting fraud through pattern recognition and anomaly detection. It doesn't just flag suspicious activity; it learns from each new fraud attempt, getting smarter over time.

Example: PayPal's fraud detection engine uses machine learning models trained on over **20 years of transaction data**, analyzing billions of transactions in real-time to prevent fraud without blocking legitimate purchases.

3. Smarter Credit Scoring

AI democratizes access to credit. Traditional credit scoring methods are often rigid, outdated, and biased. AI-based credit systems can analyze:

- Utility bill payments
- Mobile phone data
- Rental history
- Education and job stability

This gives more people - especially those in underbanked regions - a fair shot at loans and financial inclusion.

4. Personalized Financial Services

Imagine opening your banking app and it already knows what you're likely to do next - transfer money, invest, or save. AI systems can now:

- Predict user behavior
- Suggest financial products tailored to your goals
- Provide budget reminders or spending alerts

This level of personalization builds trust and enhances user experience, making finance more human - even when it's driven by machines.

The Evolution of FinTech with AI

Let's take a brief walk through time to see how we got here:

Stage 1: Digitization of Finance (Early 2000s–2010s)

The initial wave of FinTech was about **moving offline processes online**:

- Mobile banking apps
- Online money transfers
- Peer-to-peer lending platforms like LendingClub and Zopa

These were digital solutions but still based on traditional frameworks.

Stage 2: Intelligence-Driven Finance (2015–2024)

The second wave introduced **AI and machine learning**. Financial services became:

- **Smarter**: Using AI to optimize everything from credit checks to wealth management.
- **Faster**: Reducing approval times from weeks to minutes.
- **More Scalable**: Serving millions of users with minimal human oversight.

AI-enabled FinTech began to outperform traditional banks in customer acquisition, cost efficiency, and risk management.

Stage 3: Autonomous & Predictive Finance (2025 and Beyond)

Looking ahead, the next evolution will be **autonomous finance**. We'll see:

- AI managing investments with zero human input.
- Predictive banking where banks forecast needs before customers act.
- Cross-industry integration, where AI connects financial, health, and behavioral data to make holistic financial decisions.

AI will not only **respond** to your needs it will **anticipate** them.

Summary

The foundation of future financial development rests on artificial intelligence rather than serving as a simple feature. The industrial disruption affects more than just technological aspects yet extends towards fundamental principles.

Modern financial systems have transitioned from responding to rules while being reactive toward a proactive intelligent systems. The progress toward an AI-age has introduced money-related processes through learning algorithms which continuously adjust and develop themselves.

Our following section will cover how AI assists individuals with their personal finances by creating advanced methods to track and grow their money which were unthinkable before.

Chapter 2: The Rise of Smart Banking

Traditional high-street banking based on buildings and uniformed staff now represents a thing of the past. The banking sector witnesses a quick rise of smart banking which makes use of AI technologies to supply consolidated services that meet increased safety demands while providing individualized solutions to bank customers.

The application of AI technology provides banks the power to complete fraud detection instantly and also allows them to give immediate loan approvals and customized financial guidance to users. This segment explains latest banking services in smart systems and their technological foundations and explores traditional banking institutions' fight against digital transformation.

AI-Powered Banking Services: Beyond Digital, Toward Intelligent

Online banking brought a revolutionary change when it was introduced. Users gained access to balance checks and electronic bill payment and account transfers through a home computer system. The original digital banking innovations from past decades have experienced major growth into present-day advanced solutions. By bringing artificial intelligence into the picture digital banking has evolved into an advanced version called intelligent banking.

Some of the most significant breakthroughs include:

1. Real-Time Risk Assessment

AI models assess a customer's financial health instantly. Whether it's a credit card limit increase or a mortgage application, AI can evaluate income, behavior, and spending patterns far faster—and often more fairly than traditional credit checks.

2. Voice and Facial Recognition

Banks are incorporating biometric AI for **secure logins and identity verification**. HSBC, for instance, offers voice recognition that eliminates the need for passwords or PINs.

3. Dynamic Loan Approvals

Instead of relying solely on historical credit scores, AI can now assess alternative data (such as education, job history, or utility bill payments) to approve or deny loans in real time. This has helped open access to credit for millions of underbanked individuals.

4. Automated Investing and Saving Tools

Digital banking applications now consist of AI-powered functions which round up small purchase amounts for investment purposes along with generating budget recommendations and carrying out automatic savings movements according to user spending patterns.

Chime demonstrates a clear case of AI-powered management with its fee-free banking services and automatic saving features that operate from U.S. neobank infrastructure. Users gain automatic notification alerts and built-in overdraft assistance and live feed updates from this system without requiring human advisor contact.

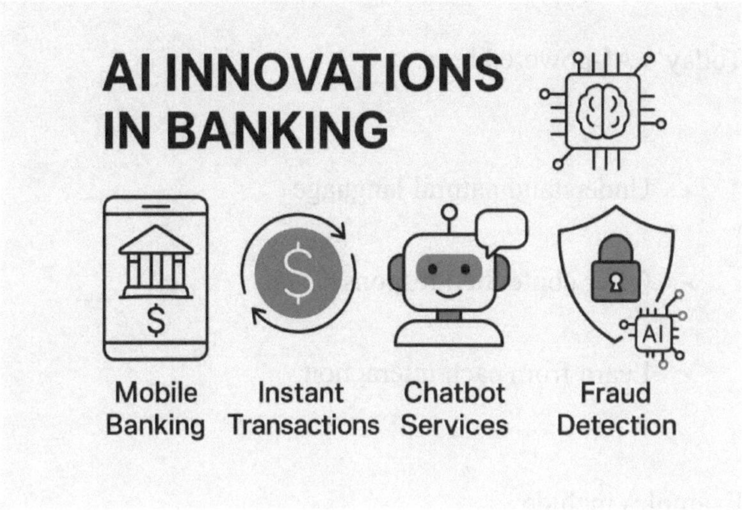

Chatbots, Fraud Detection, and Personalized Banking

Perhaps the most visible face of AI in banking today is the chatbot but there's much more going on behind the scenes.

1. Chatbots & Virtual Assistants

Chatbots have moved beyond simple scripted replies. Today's AI-powered bots:

- Understand natural language
- Offer contextual responses
- Learn from each interaction

Examples include:

- **Erica** by Bank of America: Handles tasks like bill payments, spending analysis, and transaction searches.
- **Eno** by Capital One: Detects unusual charges and offers real-time insights through SMS or app messages.

These assistants are available 24/7, reducing customer service costs while improving satisfaction.

2. Fraud Detection in Real Time

The past technique for fraud detection processed transactions using static parameters such as geographic location and monetary value and transaction frequency. AI systems review numerous transactions at once through pattern recognition to prevent fraud activities from affecting the user.

Through artificial intelligence technology JPMorgan Chase implements a system that tracks rare activities occurring throughout its customers' account network. This detection system enables the AI to discover novel fraud occurrences in brief periods while making on-the-spot parameter modifications that surpass human capability at large scales.

3. Hyper-Personalization

AI enables banks to tailor financial products, advice, and alerts based on an individual's habits. Instead of offering generic promotions, smart banks now provide:

- Personalized credit card offers
- Dynamic interest rate suggestions
- Spending insights ("You've spent 20% more on dining this month")
- Financial wellness nudges ("You're on track to save $5,000 by June!")

This level of personalization builds loyalty and creates stronger customer relationships, something traditional banks have long struggled to achieve

The Impact on Traditional Banks

The rise of AI-driven smart banking poses a critical question for legacy banks: **adapt or fall behind**.

Challenges for Traditional Banks

- **Outdated Infrastructure**: Many big banks are still built on decades-old core banking systems, making AI integration expensive and slow.
- **Cultural Resistance**: Shifting from human-led processes to AI-assisted workflows often meets internal resistance.

- **Talent Shortage**: Hiring skilled AI engineers and data scientists is competitive and many opt to join agile startups or tech-first neobanks.

Opportunities for Legacy Institutions

However, the rise of smart banking doesn't mean traditional banks are doomed. Those willing to evolve can benefit immensely by:

- Partnering with FinTech startups (as seen with Goldman Sachs and Apple Card)
- Building in-house innovation labs
- Investing in AI research and cloud-native platforms

Some institutions, like **BBVA** in Spain and **DBS Bank** in Singapore, have already made significant strides, embedding AI into customer service, lending, and compliance.

Summary

Modern banking has evolved beyond being a trend because it has established itself as the standard form of operation. AI fulfills every requirement that consumers seek regarding speed alongside convenience and personalized services. The actual transformation takes place in banking infrastructure systems where AI quietly restructures banking operations without visible human intervention. Traditional banks must display tenacity together with investments to create new systems which demand significant initiative in restructuring their operations. People using smart banking systems now operate within an environment offering safer and simpler financial services together with human-style interactions through automated systems. The following chapter investigates how algorithms construct investment portfolios while forecasting markets for universal financial growth which includes primary investors and institutional wealth management.

Chapter 3: Algorithmic Trading and AI-Driven Investments

In the rapidly evolving world of finance, artificial intelligence (AI) has emerged as a game-changer. Nowhere is this more evident than in algorithmic trading and AI-driven investments, where machines are not just assisting traders but replacing them altogether. AI is rewriting the rules of how markets move, how investments are made, and how risk is managed.

How AI is Reshaping Stock Markets

AI systems now have the power to scan millions of data points from news feeds, social media, market data, and economic indicators—analyzing and acting on that information in milliseconds. This speed and scale are far beyond human capacity. Machine learning models, particularly deep learning algorithms, are used to identify patterns and predict price movements with impressive accuracy.

Graph: Growth of AI-Driven Trading Volume Over the Last Decade

Let me show you a graph to illustrate this explosive growth:

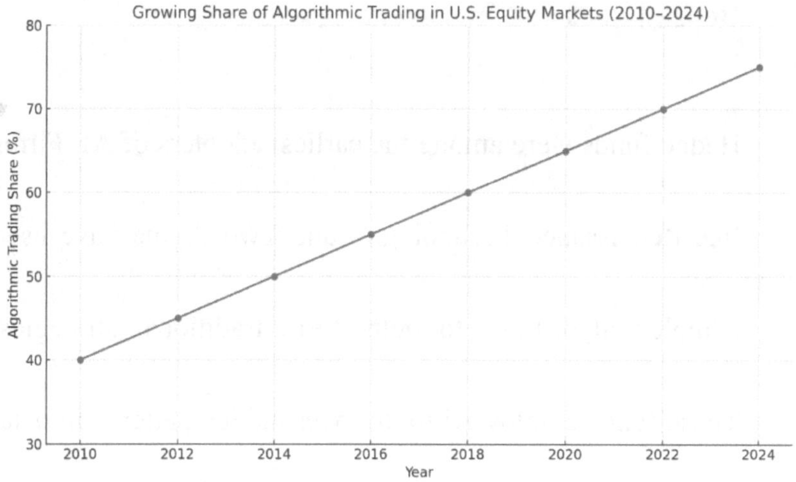

Source: U.S. Equity Markets Analysis (2024)

This graph shows the growing share of algorithmic trading in U.S. equity markets. As AI capabilities improve, its adoption across global exchanges follows suit.

The result of this advancement is a stock market that reacts faster and often more rationally—but sometimes also more erratically depending on how algorithms interpret events.

Hedge Funds and Robo-Advisors

Hedge funds were among the earliest adopters of AI. Firms like Renaissance Technologies and Two Sigma have used complex algorithms to outperform traditional strategies. These funds employ AI to discover hidden patterns in data, optimize portfolios, and execute trades with minimal latency.

On the retail side, robo-advisors are transforming how individuals invest. Platforms like Betterment and Wealthfront use AI to analyze user goals, risk tolerance, and market conditions, then construct and rebalance portfolios automatically.

An example of a user-friendly interface powered by robo-advisors using AI algorithms.

These tools provide affordable and personalized investing opportunities, making intelligent financial planning accessible to a broader audience.

The Risks and Ethics of AI in Trading

Despite the benefits, AI-driven trading isn't without its risks. "Flash crashes" caused by algorithmic misbehavior have shown how unpredictable machine-led markets can be. Since many AI models operate as "black boxes," it's often unclear why they make certain decisions - raising issues of accountability.

Ethical concerns include:

- **Bias in data**: Algorithms can inherit biases from the data they're trained on.
- **Transparency**: Traders and regulators may not understand how decisions are made.
- **Market manipulation**: AI could be used unethically to exploit market inefficiencies.

Policymakers are increasingly aware of these risks, and regulations are slowly catching up. However, as AI capabilities grow, there's a constant need to evaluate its impact on market stability and investor trust.

Summary

AI is not just a tool in financial markets, it is becoming a driving force. From institutional hedge funds to everyday investors using robo-advisors, AI is reshaping how wealth is managed and grown. Yet, as with any disruptive technology, its power must be matched with ethical oversight and thoughtful regulation.

The future will likely belong to those who can harness AI intelligently balancing innovation with integrity.

Chapter 4: AI in Risk Management and Fraud Detection

The evolution of complex electronic financial systems invites proportional growth of security risks. New techniques of internet exploitation have emerged thereby creating a necessity for modernized security measures. The critical tool which Artificial Intelligence (AI) functions as for preventing fraud and managing risks provides extraordinary speed and precision and making predictions that surpass human abilities.

This section examines AI's ability to foresee financial fraud occurrences together with its financial prevention capabilities as well as its execution in thwarting substantial attempted fraudulent activities.

How AI Predicts and Prevents Financial Fraud

Fraud detection systems of the past operated based on rules which produced flags for review after detecting specific conditions similar to excessive withdrawal limits. Yet this strategy remains beneficial yet proves reactive and rigid to the fraudster's easily achieved evasion techniques.AI, however, brings a dynamic, proactive approach:

- **Pattern Recognition:** AI can analyze vast amounts of transaction data to detect unusual patterns in real-time.
- **Anomaly Detection:** Machine learning models can distinguish between normal and abnormal behavior, flagging suspicious activities even if they don't break predefined rules.

- **Predictive Analysis:** AI can forecast potential fraud risks by learning from historical fraud cases.

For instance, AI models deployed by banks can detect subtle indicators like:

- Multiple small transactions attempting to bypass detection thresholds.
- Unusual login locations and device fingerprints.
- Changes in user behavior, such as suddenly different purchasing patterns.

These capabilities allow financial institutions to prevent fraud **before** it occurs, instead of merely reacting after the damage is done.

Graph: Rise of AI Adoption in Fraud Detection (2015–2025)

To visualize this growth, take a look at this graph showing how institutions have embraced AI for fraud detection over the past decade:

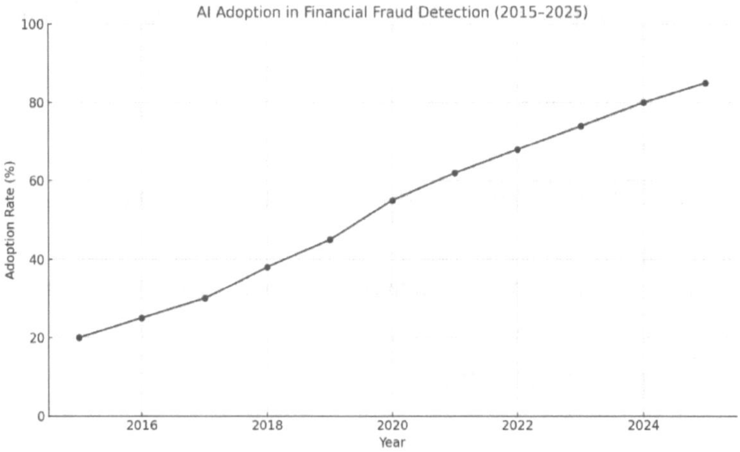

This chart highlights a major trend: in 2015, only about **20%** of major financial institutions actively used AI in fraud management. By 2025, this figure is projected to surpass

85%. Institutions now realize that without AI, they are vulnerable to increasingly sophisticated attacks.

The Role of Machine Learning in Cybersecurity

Beyond fraud detection, AI especially machine learning (ML) is playing an essential role in cybersecurity.

Here's how:

- **Threat Intelligence:** ML algorithms analyze data from across the internet (including the dark web) to predict and preempt emerging threats.
- **Intrusion Detection:** AI monitors systems for unusual activity, often detecting breaches in minutes rather than the days or weeks it takes human teams.

- **Automated Incident Response:** AI systems can automatically isolate compromised accounts or systems, mitigating damage quickly.

Zero-day threat detection finds favorable applications using deep learning models because such models find previously undetected organizational vulnerabilities. AI uses previous behaviors to discover new attack types that current antivirus technology cannot prevent but AI can detect. Working independently does not match the quick speed of modern cyber threat evolution present in today's technological environment.

Case Studies of AI Stopping Major Fraud Cases

Real-world examples show the power of AI in action:

1. **Mastercard and Brighterion AI**

Mastercard deployed Brighterion as an AI system which uses machine learning to examine hundreds of billions of transactions in current time. The implementation of Brighterion AI systems allowed their operators to reduce false positive errors by 40% while preserving customer activity integrity.

2. **HSBC's Partnership with Quantexa**

Brighterion stands as an AI system operated by Mastercard to utilize machine learning for real-time monitoring of billions of transactions. Testing demonstrated Brighterion resulted in a 40% decrease of false alarms alongside better fraud detection as well as unaltered customer operations.

3. **PayPal's Deep Learning Defense**

Deep learning networks operating at PayPal track cross-global suspicious activities on millions of accounts. The implementation resulted in a 60% increase of their fraud detection capabilities which helped them stop potential annual losses reaching billions of dollars.

The cases demonstrate how artificial intelligence accomplishes more than fraud prevention because it builds trust relationships between customers and institutions and prevents organizations from enduring substantial financial losses.

Summary

Modern-day combat against financial crimes and cyber security threats depends completely on artificial intelligence technologies. Financial institutions leverage artificial intelligence to detect incidents immediately before they create predictive models about potential threats that outperform even the most modern criminals.

The increase in AI tool strength brings a parallel increase in attackers' capability to mitigate threats. Future success hinges on two factors: constant innovation and ethical use of AI technology along with solid alliance work between institutions and technology providers and governmental regulators.

Companies that invest in Artificial Intelligence at this time achieve two objectives: they protect their financial stability while also earning customer trust which ensures the safety of digital financial services.

Chapter 5: The Future of Lending and Credit Scoring

In the traditional financial world, lending decisions have long been dominated by rigid credit scoring models—systems that often exclude millions of people from access to credit simply because their financial history doesn't fit conventional molds. Now, Artificial Intelligence is breaking those barriers, offering smarter, faster, and more inclusive approaches to lending and credit assessment.

This chapter explores how AI-driven credit assessments are revolutionizing finance, how alternative data is promoting broader financial inclusion, and how new AI-powered lending platforms are reshaping the borrowing experience.

AI-Driven Credit Assessments

Traditionally, credit scores like FICO or VantageScore have been based on a narrow range of factors:

- Payment history
- Outstanding debt
- Length of credit history
- Types of credit used
- New credit inquiries

While effective to a degree, these models are simplistic, inflexible, and often outdated in today's fast-moving economy. AI changes the game.

How AI Enhances Credit Assessment:

- **Multidimensional Analysis:** AI can consider hundreds or thousands of data points beyond traditional metrics.
- **Real-Time Decisioning:** AI enables lenders to make faster lending decisions, sometimes in seconds.
- **Behavioral Analytics:** Machine learning models assess not just financial data but behavioral patterns (e.g., spending habits, utility payments, rental history).
- **Continuous Learning:** Unlike static models, AI systems continuously learn and adapt to new borrower behaviors and economic conditions.

With AI, credit assessment becomes more accurate, dynamic, and predictive. It's no longer about what you did five years ago it's about how you behave today and how likely you are to repay tomorrow.

Graph: Global AI in Credit Scoring Market Growth (2020–2030)

Let's visualize how fast AI is being adopted in the credit scoring industry:

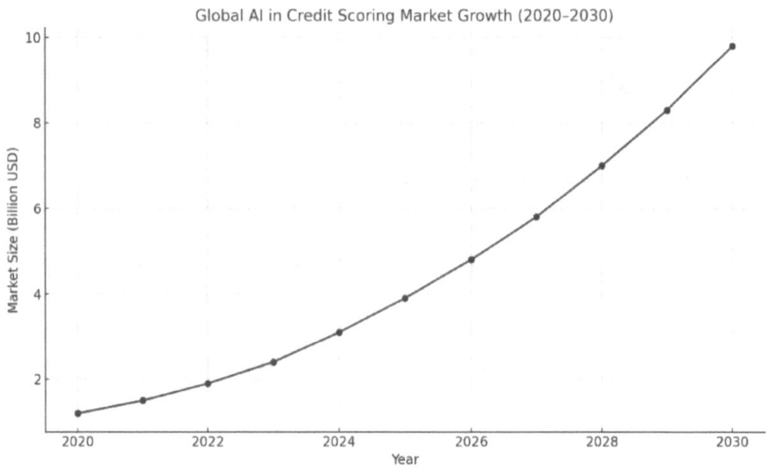

This graph will show the global market size for AI in credit scoring, illustrating how AI is becoming central to the future of lending decisions.

Alternative Data for Better Financial Inclusion

One of the most powerful impacts of AI-driven lending is its ability to use **alternative data** to assess creditworthiness, helping millions who were previously "credit invisible."

Examples of Alternative Data Sources:

- Rent and utility payment history
- Mobile phone bill payments
- E-commerce transactions
- Social media behavior (in certain markets)
- Education and employment history

- Savings patterns

By analyzing these data points, AI can:

- Identify financially responsible individuals who might not have traditional credit histories.
- Offer fairer, more personalized lending products.
- Reduce systemic biases embedded in traditional credit systems.

Financial Inclusion in Action: Companies like **Tala**, **Branch**, and **Kiva** are using alternative data to offer microloans to individuals in emerging markets who would otherwise have no access to formal banking services.

In developed markets, even major players like **FICO** are now experimenting with "UltraFICO," which factors in banking activity like savings patterns to improve credit scores.

This trend is closing the credit gap and giving millions of new borrowers a chance to participate in the formal economy.

The Rise of AI-Powered Lending Platforms

The new generation of lenders isn't a row of bankers in suits it's cloud-based, algorithm-driven, and highly automated. AI-powered lending platforms are revolutionizing the entire loan process:

Key Features of AI-Powered Lenders:

- **Instant Approvals:** Automated underwriting processes approve loans in minutes.

- **Personalized Offers:** Machine learning models tailor loan terms to individual borrower profiles.
- **Dynamic Risk Pricing:** Interest rates adjust based on real-time risk analysis, not outdated credit scores.
- **Fraud Detection:** AI simultaneously screens for fraud risk during the application process.

Examples of Leading AI Lending Platforms:

- **Upstart:** Uses non-traditional variables like education and employment history to predict default risks more accurately.
- **Kabbage:** Provides small business loans with minimal paperwork and AI-driven approvals.

- **Zest AI:** Helps banks and credit unions adopt AI underwriting models to improve accuracy and reduce bias.

The result? Faster loans, more customized products, and a fairer system that rewards responsible behavior, not just historical privilege.

Graph: AI-Driven Lending Volume Growth (2018–2028)

Another way to appreciate the scale of change is by looking at AI-driven lending volumes:

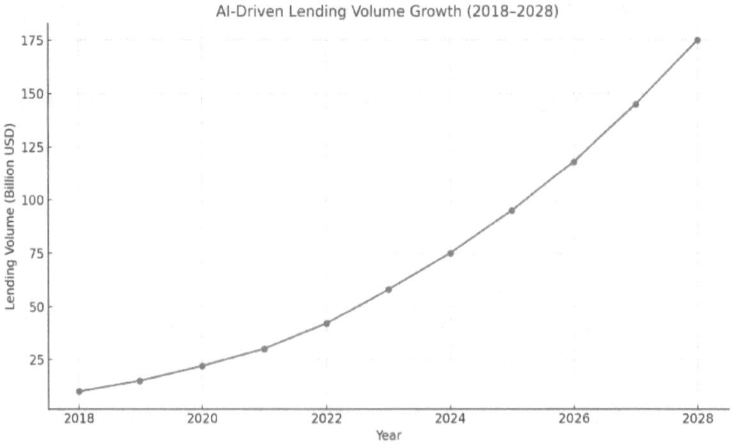

It will show how loans issued through AI-powered platforms have exploded over the past decade, highlighting the growing trust in automated credit decisioning.

Summary

Mastercard deployed Brighterion as an AI system which uses machine learning to examine hundreds of billions of transactions in current time. The system completed 40% fewer false positives while maintaining high detection accuracy throughout all updates to regular operations. The AI system Brighterion by Mastercard utilizes machine learning to supervise billions of transactions at present times. Testing demonstrated Brighterion resulted in a 40% decrease of false alarms alongside better fraud detection as well as unaltered customer operations.

Chapter 6: Decentralized Finance (DeFi) and AI

During recent years the financial industry experienced an enormous transformation toward decentralization as DeFi (decentralized finance) replaced conventional banking infrastructure.

The blockchain foundation of DeFi allows users to benefit from financial services thatPasswordFieldLeverages Blockchain to Create Neurocognitive Decentralized Network Transactions do not require authorization and function throughout the world.

Artificial Intelligence (AI) increases the potential of DeFi even more which adds optimization capabilities along with intelligence features and automation to the innovative field.

The following section examines how AI optimizes blockchain and DeFi alongside the capabilities of smart contracts and automated financial solutions whereas it also addresses the developing security warnings and upcoming AI trends regarding DeFi.

How AI is Optimizing Blockchain and DeFi

At first glance, blockchain and AI might seem like separate worlds.

Blockchain is about transparency and decentralization; AI thrives on data centralization and pattern recognition. But when combined thoughtfully, they create **a synergy that solves some of the biggest pain points in DeFi**.

Here's how AI optimizes DeFi:

- **Transaction Optimization:** AI algorithms can predict congestion on blockchain networks like Ethereum and help users minimize gas fees by choosing the best transaction timing.
- **Liquidity Management:** DeFi platforms use AI to automate and balance liquidity pools, ensuring users have access to funds without excessive slippage or volatility.
- **Risk Assessment:** AI evaluates borrowers' behavior and trading activity in decentralized lending markets to detect fraud and assess creditworthiness—without needing traditional credit reports.
- **Market Prediction:** Machine learning models analyze market sentiment across news feeds, social

media, and transaction histories to predict price movements in decentralized assets.

Without AI, DeFi could easily become chaotic and inefficient.

With AI, it becomes smarter, faster, and much more user-friendly.

Table: How AI Enhances Key Areas of DeFi

DeFi Application	AI Enhancement	Real-World Example
Lending Platforms	Risk scoring using alternative data	Aave AI credit scoring

Decentralized Exchanges (DEXs)	Price prediction and liquidity management	Uniswap V3 dynamic fee models
Yield Farming	Optimal reward strategies	Yearn.Finance yield optimization
Blockchain Security	Threat detection and anomaly spotting	OpenZeppelin AI auditing tools
NFT Marketplaces	Fraud detection and authenticity verification	OpenSea fraud prevention AI

This table shows just a snapshot of how AI is already weaving itself into every corner of the DeFi universe. And we're still at the beginning.

Smart Contracts and Automated Financial Services

At the heart of DeFi are **smart contracts** self-executing agreements written in code that run automatically when certain conditions are met. But AI is making smart contracts even smarter.

Here's how AI improves smart contracts:

- **Dynamic Execution:** Traditional smart contracts follow rigid rules. AI-enhanced contracts can adapt based on real-world conditions, like adjusting loan interest rates based on market volatility.

- **Error Detection:** AI can audit smart contracts before deployment, identifying bugs, vulnerabilities, or logic errors that human developers might miss.
- **Automated Arbitration:** In disputes, AI systems can act as decentralized arbitrators, analyzing evidence and executing fair outcomes without human bias.

In a real-world scenario, imagine a DeFi insurance contract that automatically assesses natural disaster data from satellites. If a flood occurs in a specific area, the contract pays out instantly—no claim forms, no middlemen.

That's not science fiction anymore. Projects like **Nexus Mutual** and **Etherisc** are already building toward that future.

Graph: Growth of AI Integration in DeFi Projects (2019–2025)

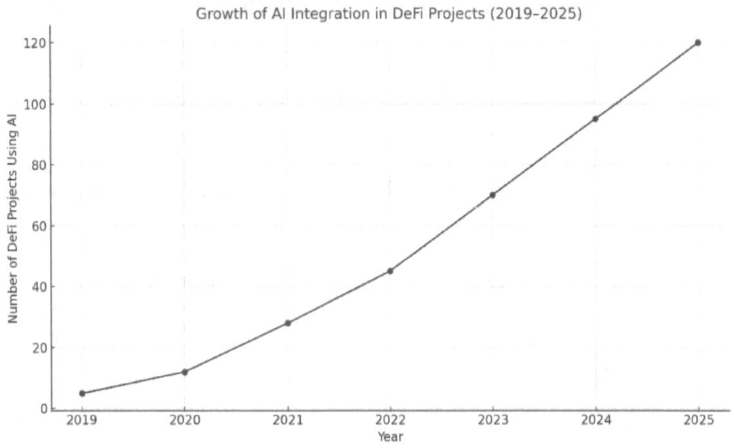

To understand how fast AI is being adopted in the DeFi world, look at this graph showing the number of DeFi projects actively integrating AI technologies: You'll see a clear surge - AI is no longer an optional "nice to have" in DeFi; it's becoming a necessity.

Risks and Future Trends in AI-Driven DeFi

While the potential is enormous, AI-driven DeFi also introduces new risks we can't ignore:

Key Risks:

- **Algorithmic Bias:** If AI models are trained on biased data, they can perpetuate or even amplify inequalities.
- **Security Flaws:** Hackers could exploit vulnerabilities not just in smart contracts, but in the AI algorithms themselves.
- **Autonomy Without Oversight:** Fully autonomous financial systems could behave unpredictably,

leading to catastrophic outcomes if not properly monitored.

- **Regulatory Grey Areas:** DeFi itself challenges regulatory frameworks. Adding AI to the mix makes oversight even more complex.

Despite these risks, the future looks bright for AI in DeFi.

Emerging Trends to Watch:

- **Self-Evolving Smart Contracts:** Contracts that adjust based on new conditions without needing redeployment.
- **DeFi Credit Bureaus:** Decentralized, AI-driven profiles assessing borrowers without the need for invasive background checks.

- **Cross-Chain AI Agents:** AI systems that operate across multiple blockchains seamlessly, optimizing liquidity and arbitrage.
- **AI Governance:** Decentralized Autonomous Organizations (DAOs) managed by AI agents instead of human votes.

The DeFi space will reward those who balance innovation with responsibility - those who build not just smarter systems, but fairer and safer ones too.

Summary

DeFi brings forth the most significant financial revolution since the start of the twentieth century.

The acceleration of that financial system reimagination happens through Artificial Intelligence which provides blockchain-based finance with intelligence and adaptability and inclusiveness properties. The path toward this transition requires proper leadership.

When implemented correctly the alliance of AI technology with DeFi protocols can develop a financial structure that surpasses every system we have known thus far. The path ahead is just beginning with DeFi and its fusion power because individuals who grasp the vital role of this combination will forge the financial direction for approaching ages.

Chapter 7: InsurTech - How AI is Reshaping the Insurance Industry

Insurance is one of civilization's oldest industries, built on assessing risk and offering protection. Yet today, it's undergoing a historic shift - fueled by Artificial Intelligence that's redefining everything from underwriting to claims to pricing. What was once slow, paperwork-heavy, and based on averages is becoming **real-time, predictive, and personalized**. In this chapter, we'll explore how AI is revolutionizing insurance through **risk assessment**, **claims automation**, and **dynamic pricing models**, and why it matters more than ever.

AI-Powered Risk Assessment

Traditionally, insurers evaluated risk using broad demographic data - age, gender, location to set rates. But this approach often missed the nuances of individual behavior.

AI changes the game.

Now, insurers gather **millions of real-time data points** from telematics, wearable devices, and IoT (Internet of Things) sensors to create **dynamic, hyper-personalized** risk profiles.

Key components include:

- **Continuous Data Collection:** Smartwatches, connected cars, and home sensors provide constant updates.
- **Predictive Analytics:** AI models detect patterns that suggest future risks before problems even occur.
- **Dynamic Risk Scoring:** Risk profiles adjust continuously based on new data, not just once a year at policy renewal.

Imagine earning a lower health insurance premium immediately because your fitness tracker shows improved exercise habits or your car insurance dropping after a month of safer driving. Companies like Root Insurance and

Lemonade are already pioneering this personalized approach.

Table: Traditional vs. AI-Powered Risk Assessment

Feature	Traditional Model	AI-Enhanced Model
Data Sources	Static, historical data	Real-time, continuous data
Risk Segmentation	Broad demographics	Individual behavior patterns

Frequency of Updates	Annual or semi-annual	Continuous and dynamic
Level of Personalization	Low	High
Predictive Capability	Reactive (after event)	Predictive (before event)

AI-driven risk assessment doesn't just speed up decisions—it makes them smarter and more **individually relevant**.

Automation in Claims and Underwriting

Claims processing and underwriting have long been **the most frustrating parts** of insurance for customers. Lengthy forms, phone calls, manual verification - it's an experience few would describe as seamless.

Enter AI.

Here's how it transforms the process:

- **Image Recognition:** AI tools like Tractable analyze damage photos instantly to estimate repair costs.
- **Natural Language Processing (NLP):** Smart chatbots gather claim details and submit reports without human assistance.
- **Automated Underwriting:** AI reviews applications, financial records, and medical histories to approve or deny coverage within minutes - sometimes seconds.

One standout case: Lemonade Insurance processed a claim in just 3 seconds a record-setting demonstration of automation at work.

Graph: Average Time to Process an Insurance Claim (Traditional vs. AI-Enhanced)

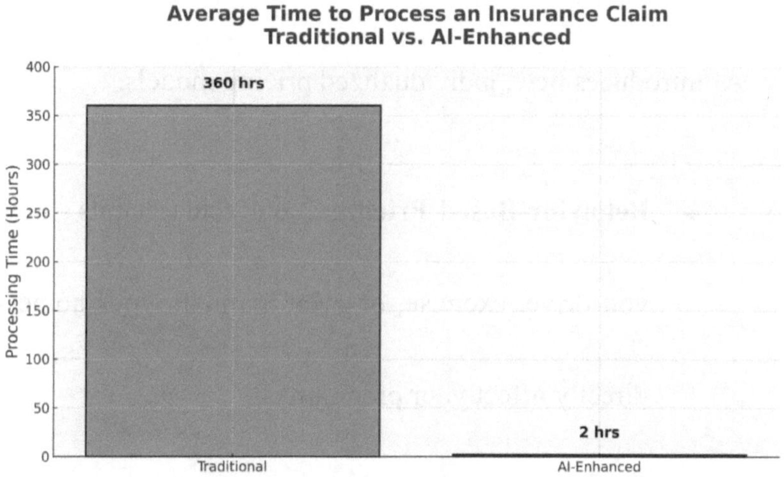

How AI is Revolutionizing Pricing Models

Insurance pricing was once based on group averages: Find your demographic → Assign you to a category → Charge you accordingly.

AI introduces new, individualized pricing models:

- **Behavior-Based Pricing:** Your actual habits - how you drive, exercise, or even maintain your home - directly affect your premiums.
- **Dynamic Pricing:** Insurance costs can adjust monthly, weekly, or even daily based on updated risk profiles.

- **Microinsurance:** Short-term, event-specific coverage (e.g., travel insurance that activates automatically when your flight leaves).

Imagine seeing your premium **drop instantly** because you drove less at night this month or improved your blood pressure. The result? Insurance that's more **transparent, fair, and motivating**.

Real-World Examples

- **Root Insurance:** Pricing based primarily on driving behavior, not demographics.
- **Tractable:** Uses AI to speed up car damage assessments, cutting claim times by 70%.

- **Shift Technology:** Detects insurance fraud patterns using AI with greater accuracy than traditional methods.

These examples show that **AI isn't just an upgrade it's a complete rethinking** of how insurance can work.

Challenges and Ethical Considerations

Of course, with great power comes responsibility. AI-driven insurance faces critical challenges:

- **Bias in AI:** Algorithms trained on biased data can unintentionally reinforce discrimination.
- **Privacy Risks:** Continuous data collection raises major concerns about user consent and data security.

- **Transparency:** Many customers don't fully understand how AI decisions are made, leading to potential distrust.

To truly improve insurance, companies must commit to ethical AI: fair, unbiased, and respectful of user privacy.

Summary

Artificial Intelligence is not just modernizing insurance, it's reinventing it.

With smarter risk models, faster claims, and more personalized pricing, AI promises an insurance experience that's fairer, faster, and more human-centered.

But this revolution must be built on ethical foundations. The insurers who balance innovation with responsibility will earn the greatest rewards and the trust of tomorrow's customers.

Chapter 8: AI and Financial Regulations

As artificial intelligence (AI) transforms the world of finance, it's also rewriting the rulebook for how financial institutions stay compliant, secure, and ethical. The integration of AI into banking, trading, lending, and wealth management brings unparalleled speed and sophistication but it also creates new regulatory challenges that governments and watchdogs are racing to address.

In this chapter, we explore the role of AI in regulatory compliance (RegTech), the challenges regulators face, and the ethical concerns that arise as finance becomes increasingly AI-led.

AI's Role in Regulatory Compliance (RegTech)

Regulatory Technology (RegTech) refers to the use of technology to help companies comply with regulations efficiently and at lower cost.

AI has supercharged RegTech solutions, making them smarter, faster, and more predictive.

Here's how AI is reshaping compliance:

- **Automated Monitoring:**

  AI systems can scan millions of transactions in real time, detecting suspicious patterns that humans might miss.

- **Risk Management:**

  Machine learning models assess credit, market, and operational risks with unprecedented precision.

- **Fraud Detection:**

  AI can identify anomalies and unusual behavior, enabling faster action against money laundering, insider trading, and cybercrime.

- **Regulatory Reporting:**

  Natural Language Processing (NLP) tools automatically extract, organize, and submit required reports to regulators - reducing manual errors.

- **Smart Audits:**

  AI assists in reviewing records and contracts for compliance breaches or inconsistencies, making audits more thorough and efficient.

Real-world examples:

- **Ayasdi:** Uses AI to detect financial crimes and hidden risks in banking systems.
- **ComplyAdvantage:** Leverages AI to monitor financial crimes globally and flag high-risk transactions.

Table: Traditional Compliance vs AI-Driven RegTech

Feature	Traditional Compliance	AI-Powered RegTech
Data Processing Speed	Slow, manual reviews	Real-time, automated analysis

Error Rate	High (human error prone)	Low (machine learning optimized)
Scalability	Limited	High (big data processing)
Adaptability to New Rules	Slow, costly updates	Dynamic, continuous updates

Cost	High (labor intensive)	Lower (automation-driven)

As shown above, AI doesn't just make compliance faster - it makes it smarter, cheaper, and far more scalable.

Challenges of AI-Driven Finance for Regulators

As financial institutions adopt AI, regulators face a growing list of challenges:

- **Opacity ('Black Box' Problem):**

  Many AI models are so complex that even their

creators struggle to explain how decisions are made. This lack of transparency makes oversight difficult.

- **Privacy and Data Security Risks:**

  AI systems require massive amounts of sensitive data, raising concerns about how customer information is collected, stored, and protected.

- **Pace of Technological Change:**

  Regulators often move slower than tech innovation. By the time regulations are updated, AI systems have already evolved.

- **Bias and Fairness:**

  If AI models are trained on biased data, they can reinforce discrimination - leading to unfair credit decisions, investment advice, or risk assessments.

- **Cross-Border Challenges:**

  Finance is global, but regulations are local. Creating consistent AI standards across different countries is extremely complicated.

Graph: Regulator Challenges in AI-Driven Finance

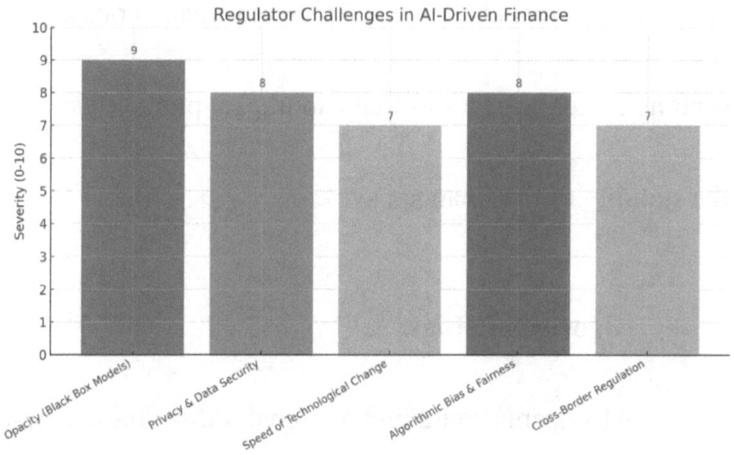

This graph shows the severity of different challenges regulators face when overseeing AI in finance, rated on a scale from 1 (low severity) to 10 (high severity).

- Opacity scored the highest, reflecting deep concerns about "black box" AI.
- Privacy and Bias also rank high, emphasizing ongoing ethical and data protection issues.

Ethical Concerns in AI-Led Finance

Beyond technical challenges, AI-driven finance raises **serious ethical questions** that can impact public trust and the stability of the financial system:

- **Algorithmic Bias:**

  AI systems could unintentionally discriminate based on race, gender, age, or socioeconomic status—especially in areas like lending or insurance underwriting.

- **Lack of Transparency:**

  Customers may not understand why they were denied a loan, offered a lower credit limit, or given unfavorable investment advice if AI models are too opaque.

- **Accountability:**

  If an AI makes a wrong or harmful decision, who is responsible? The bank? The tech provider? The AI developer? These questions remain unresolved.

- **Surveillance Risks:**

  AI enables mass data collection and profiling, risking intrusive surveillance practices under the guise of "risk management."

- **Exacerbation of Inequality:**

  There is a risk that wealthy, tech-savvy users will benefit the most from AI-enhanced financial services, widening the gap between financial "haves" and "have-nots."

Summary

AI is not just tweaking the financial system - it's fundamentally redefining it. Regulators, compliance officers, and financial firms must work hand-in-hand to harness AI's advantages while **managing its risks** thoughtfully.

Smart RegTech tools offer better compliance, cheaper operations, and faster reporting.

However, without proper guardrails, AI could entrench bias, violate privacy, and destabilize global markets.

The future of AI in finance depends on balance:

- Innovation must be matched with regulation.
- Speed must be tempered with scrutiny.
- Profit must be pursued ethically.

In short, as financial AI grows smarter, regulators must grow wiser.

Only then can the financial system remain not only efficient but also fair, transparent, and trusted.

Chapter 9: AI in Wealth Management and Personalized Finance

The financial world has historically been reserved for those with significant assets and insider knowledge. Access to personal financial advisors, wealth managers, and customized investment strategies was a privilege of the affluent.

But with the rise of **AI** the world of **wealth management** and personalized finance has been democratized. Today, intelligent algorithms can deliver personalized advice, tailored savings plans, and sophisticated investment strategies to virtually anyone with a smartphone — in real time.

In this chapter, we'll explore how AI is revolutionizing:

- Financial planning
- Budgeting and saving behaviors
- The psychological impact of AI-driven financial decisions

How AI Tailors Financial Planning

Traditional financial planning was static: You'd meet with an advisor once a year, fill out a paper survey about your goals, and get a general plan based on broad models. AI **has** shattered that mold. Now, financial planning is dynamic, continuous, and hyper-personalized.

Here's how AI transforms financial planning:

- **Real-Time Data Integration:** AI systems pull data from banking apps, spending habits, investment portfolios, credit reports, even social media to get a full view of your financial life.
- **Predictive Analytics:** AI doesn't just assess where you are — it predicts where you're likely headed financially, spotting risks and opportunities early.
- **Behavioral Insights:** Machine learning algorithms adapt recommendations based on your unique behaviors — whether you're a spender, a saver, a risk-taker, or conservative.

Imagine an AI advisor that notices you've received a work bonus and instantly suggests how to invest it, pay down debt, or save it for a future goal.

Platforms like Wealthfront, Betterment, Finnimo and Ellevest are already using AI to create highly customized financial plans for millions of users.

Graph 1: Traditional Financial Planning vs. AI-Driven Planning

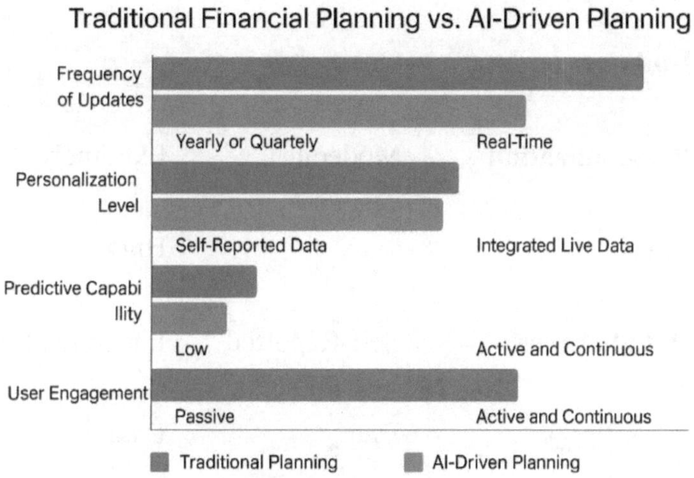

Graph 1: Traditional Financial Planning vs. AI-Driven Planning

Feature	Traditional Planning	AI-Driven Planning
Frequency of Updates	Yearly or Quarterly	Real-Time
Personalization Level	Moderate	Extremely High
Data Sources	Self-Reported Data	Integrated Live Data
Predictive Capability	Low	High
User Engagement	Passive	Active and Continuous

*(This table highlights how much more **dynamic** and **responsive** AI-based planning has become.)*

AI-Based Budgeting and Saving Assistants

Saving money and sticking to a budget has always been a challenge even for the financially disciplined. Impulse purchases, unexpected expenses, and poor forecasting often derail the best-laid plans.

Enter AI budgeting and saving assistants.

These digital tools powered by machine learning help users make smarter day-to-day decisions without overwhelming them with complexity.

Key features of AI saving assistants:

- **Spending Pattern Analysis:** AI tracks your habits and automatically identifies unnecessary expenses.
- **Smart Budget Creation:** Instead of static budgets, AI adapts your budget monthly, based on your real-time income and spending.
- **Automated Savings:** Some apps automatically move small amounts of money into savings based on what you can afford that day (e.g., **Digit** and **Qapital**).
- **Goal Optimization:** Whether it's a vacation, a wedding, or retirement, AI recommends the best savings strategies tailored to your timeline and budget.

For example, if your income suddenly dips, your AI assistant can immediately lower your discretionary spending allowance - preventing you from going into debt.

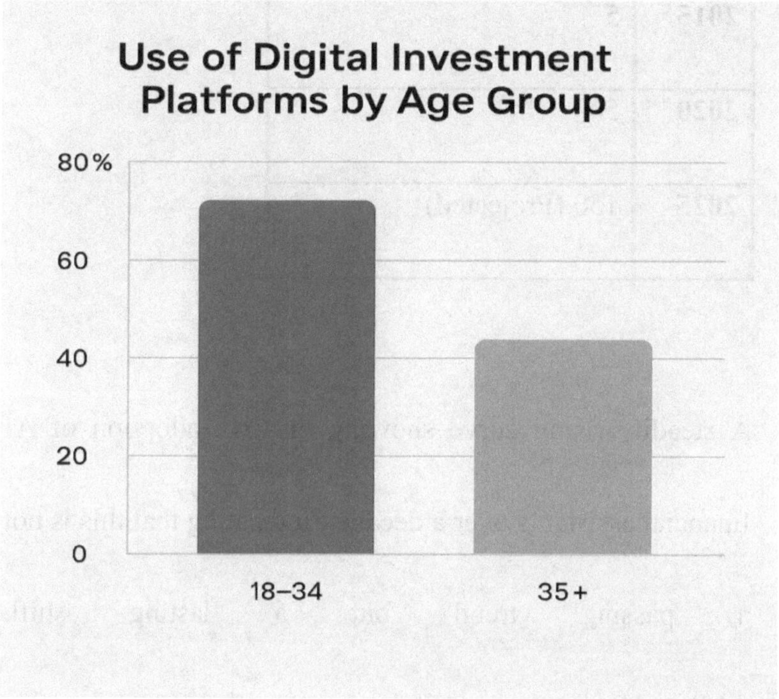

Graph 2: Growth of AI-Based Financial Assistants (2015–2025 Projection)

Year	Estimated Users (Millions)
2015	5
2020	50
2025	150 (Projected)

A steadily rising curve showing massive adoption of AI financial assistants over a decade - indicating that this is not a passing trend but a lasting shift. AI-based assistants aren't just apps - they are becoming **personal financial partners** for millions, especially **Millennials** and **Gen Z**, who prefer "self-service" advice over traditional advisors.

The Psychology of AI-Driven Financial Decisions

Money is emotional. We like to think we're rational about it - but countless studies show that humans often make irrational financial decisions based on fear, greed, excitement, or guilt.

AI helps manage these biases in powerful ways.

Psychological advantages of AI-driven finance:

- **Objective Decision-Making:** AI removes emotional reactions like panic selling during market downturns.
- **Behavioral Nudges:** Apps can gently "nudge" you toward better behaviors - like saving more or avoiding impulsive spending.

- **Gamification:** Many AI tools use progress tracking, streaks, and small rewards to make saving and investing more engaging.
- **Reduction of Decision Fatigue:** By automating routine tasks (e.g., saving, investing), AI frees up mental energy for more important decisions.

Bonus Table: Common Financial Biases & How AI Counters Them

Human Bias	Typical Behavior	How AI Helps Correct It
Loss Aversion	Selling stocks at a loss	Provides data-driven reassurances

Overconfidence	Risky investments	Recommends diversified portfolios
Present Bias	Overspending now vs. saving later	Smart goal setting & nudges
Herd Behavior	Following the crowd blindly	Customized, independent advice

Real-World Impact: Case Studies

- **Wealthfront:** Uses AI to automatically rebalance portfolios, harvest tax losses, and predict cash needs for clients.
- **Cleosave:** An AI chatbot that analyzes your spending, makes jokes, and encourages saving in a playful, psychologically savvy way.
- **Plum:** A UK-based AI assistant that reviews your accounts daily and squirrels away small amounts you won't miss.

These companies show that **intelligent, behaviorally aware** finance tools are **redefining** the customer experience - making financial literacy and wellness accessible for everyone.

Challenges and Ethical Considerations

Despite the enormous promise, AI-driven finance isn't without risks:

- **Over-Automation:** Too much reliance on AI could make users disengaged from understanding their own finances.
- **Bias in Algorithms:** If AI models are trained on biased historical financial data, they could disadvantage certain groups.
- **Privacy Concerns:** Sensitive financial data must be protected rigorously against breaches or misuse.

- **Over-Personalization Risks:** Nudges and micro-targeted recommendations could unintentionally exploit vulnerable users.

The future of personalized finance must balance **automation** with **transparency**, **privacy**, and **ethical responsibility**.

Summary

AI is not just adding convenience to financial management - it's **transforming the very psychology** of how people save, invest, and build wealth. By providing real-time insights, adapting dynamically to changing behaviors, and helping users overcome psychological barriers, AI is making personalized finance **smarter**, more humane, and more inclusive.

In the years to come, the best financial advisors may not be human at all - they may be intelligent, empathetic algorithms that understand us better than we understand ourselves. The wealth revolution has already begun. And with AI at the helm, it’s steering toward a **future where** financial security is within everyone's reach.

Chapter 10: The Dark Side of AI in Finance

Artificial Intelligence (AI) has become a powerful force in transforming the financial sector, revolutionizing everything from customer service to investment strategies. AI-driven tools now manage billions of dollars, assess credit risk in milliseconds, and predict market movements with unprecedented accuracy. But behind the promise of efficiency and profit lies a more troubling reality: AI introduces new types of risks, ethical challenges, and potential systemic threats that could have far-reaching consequences.

This chapter delves deep into the lesser-discussed dangers of AI in finance. We will explore the persistence of biases in AI systems, ethical dilemmas around fairness and accountability, the risks of over-reliance on these technologies, and the looming threat of AI-driven financial crises. As we stand at the crossroads of innovation and responsibility, understanding these issues is vital to ensure that AI serves as a tool for progress rather than a catalyst for disaster.

AI Biases and Ethical Dilemmas

AI is often touted as objective and impartial, but in reality, it reflects the imperfections of the human world. The data used to train AI systems are historical and frequently embedded with biases whether cultural, racial, gender-based, or socio-economic. When AI learns from such biased data, it risks reinforcing and even magnifying discriminatory practices.

For example, a 2018 MIT study found that facial recognition systems misidentified women and people of color at significantly higher rates than white men, raising alarms about AI fairness across industries. In finance, this issue is even more critical. Discriminatory lending practices can deny marginalized groups access to essential financial services, deepening social inequities.

The 2019 Apple Card controversy serves as a case in point. Despite having similar financial profiles, women were consistently offered lower credit limits than men. Investigators found that the AI model used for credit scoring had absorbed historical patterns of gender-based discrimination. This case fueled widespread debate about the ethical responsibility of tech firms and financial institutions in auditing their AI systems.

Beyond biases, AI's "black box" nature where algorithms make decisions without offering clear explanations poses severe challenges. This opacity can obstruct regulators from understanding how financial decisions are made, undermining transparency and trust. The European Union's General Data Protection Regulation (GDPR) has already flagged these issues, mandating a “right to explanation” when individuals are subjected to automated decisions.

Another ethical concern is data privacy. Financial AI systems require access to vast amounts of sensitive data, raising fears of breaches, misuse, and surveillance. The Cambridge Analytica scandal, though not financial, underscored the catastrophic consequences of lax data governance.

Experts argue that without robust ethical frameworks, AI could entrench systemic injustices rather than resolve them. As Cathy O'Neil, author of *Weapons of Math Destruction*, puts it: “Algorithms are opinions embedded in code.”

Risks of Over-Reliance on AI in Finance

AI's remarkable capabilities have fostered a growing dependence within financial institutions. While automation can reduce human error and increase efficiency, over-reliance on AI introduces critical vulnerabilities. The more financial systems lean on AI, the higher the stakes when something goes wrong.

The 2010 "Flash Crash" is often cited as a cautionary tale. High-frequency trading algorithms, designed to execute trades in microseconds, reacted to market signals in a feedback loop that caused the Dow Jones to plummet nearly 1,000 points in minutes. Though the market corrected itself by the end of the day, the crash wiped out $1 trillion in market capitalization—highlighting the potential for AI systems to exacerbate market volatility.

Similarly, during the COVID-19 pandemic, several AI-driven hedge funds underperformed dramatically. Their models, trained on historical data, failed to predict the unprecedented market disruptions caused by a global health crisis. These failures exposed a critical weakness: AI models excel in stable environments but can falter when faced with truly novel situations. Moreover, AI's complexity creates a significant challenge for regulators. Many advanced models, particularly those based on deep learning, evolve continuously and autonomously. This dynamic nature makes it difficult for regulators to audit or even understand the algorithms in real time. As AI systems become more ingrained in the financial sector, the lack of human oversight can allow small errors to snowball into full-blown crises. Some experts warn of the "automation bias," a cognitive bias where humans place excessive trust in automated decisions. A 2021 study by the Bank of International Settlements found that traders were more likely to overlook anomalies when algorithms were in charge, exacerbating risks of undetected failures.

Category	Description	Example
Bias in Decision-Making	AI systems may perpetuate or amplify social and economic biases, leading to unfair outcomes.	Apple Card credit limit gender bias (2019).
Lack of Transparency	Black-box algorithms obscure how decisions are made, limiting accountability and user trust.	Opaque AI credit scoring models.

Over-Reliance	Excessive dependence on AI can foster complacency and increase systemic vulnerabilities.	2010 Flash Crash triggered by algorithmic trading.
Cybersecurity Threats	AI systems are attractive targets for sophisticated cyberattacks, risking widespread financial disruption.	Hypothetical AI-driven payment system breach.
Herding Behavior	Similar AI models making identical decisions can amplify volatility and cause synchronized market moves.	2018 Volmageddon event.
Regulatory Challenges	Rapid AI innovation often outpaces regulatory frameworks, leaving oversight gaps.	Delayed response to AI-powered fintech products.

The Potential for AI-Driven Financial Crises

As AI becomes a cornerstone of global finance, its potential to trigger or amplify financial crises cannot be ignored. The interconnected nature of modern financial systems means that a failure in one AI component could ripple across institutions, markets, and borders.

The Financial Stability Board's 2023 report emphasized that AI systems particularly those used in trading, risk assessment, and liquidity management pose systemic risks if not properly regulated. The report recommended rigorous stress testing and the development of "kill switches" that can halt AI operations during emergencies.

One theoretical but highly concerning risk is the "AI feedback loop." Imagine a scenario where multiple AI-driven hedge funds, all using similar models, begin to offload assets in response to a market signal. Their collective actions could create a self-reinforcing cycle of selling, spiraling into a market crash. This is not mere speculation; during the 2018 “Volmageddon” event, the simultaneous unwinding of volatility-related investments many guided by automated systems triggered sharp market declines.

Another growing concern is cyber warfare. As AI systems handle more critical financial infrastructure, they become attractive targets for cyberattacks. A sophisticated attack on AI-driven payment systems, trading platforms, or credit networks could paralyze economies. Experts from the World

Economic Forum have warned that the next major financial crisis might not stem from traditional economic factors but from a massive cybersecurity breach.

The graph below highlights major AI-driven financial market disruptions between 2010 and 2025, illustrating how these events have shaped concerns about systemic risk:

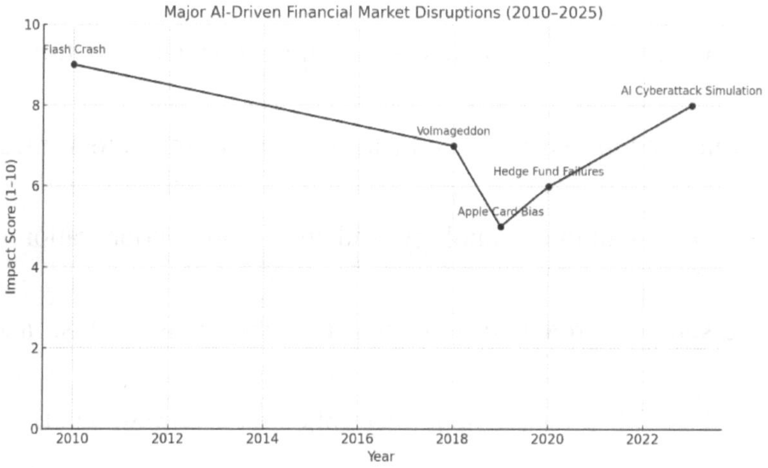

Summary

AI offers transformative potential, but its integration into the financial system is a double-edged sword. The very features that make AI attractive speed, complexity, and autonomy also make it risky. Biases in data, opaque algorithms, over-reliance, and systemic vulnerabilities could all converge to create crises of a new kind.

To harness AI's benefits responsibly, financial institutions must adopt stringent ethical standards, regulators must evolve with the technology, and cross-border cooperation is essential. Proactive governance, continuous audits, and robust fail-safes are no longer optional they are imperative.

The future of AI in finance is a delicate balancing act. If we succeed, AI can be a force for inclusivity, efficiency, and growth. If we fail, we risk building a financial system that is faster and smarter but also far more fragile.

Chapter 11: The Future of AI in FinTech

Artificial Intelligence (AI) has already left a powerful imprint on the financial world — from algorithmic trading to personalized wealth management. Yet, what we've seen so far is merely the beginning. In this chapter, we'll explore where AI is heading in finance, predictions for the next decade, and how businesses and individuals can smartly prepare for the era of AI-led financial innovation.

Where AI is Heading in Finance

The future trajectory of AI in finance promises to be even more disruptive and transformative. Several key trends are shaping its next phase:

1. Hyper-Personalization of Financial Services

AI is moving toward **real-time, individualized** financial experiences. Future banking apps and investment platforms will act more like **personal** CFOs, using deep learning to anticipate financial needs before the user even realizes them. They will manage budgets, suggest investments, optimize taxes, and even advise on lifestyle choices, all tailored at a micro-level.

2. Predictive Analytics at Scale

Instead of simply analyzing historical data, AI will proactively **forecast** financial risks, investment opportunities, and market movements with stunning precision. Imagine algorithms that not only predict recessions but also suggest personalized "recession-proof" strategies well in advance.

3. Autonomous Finance

We are entering an era of **"self-driving finance"** where systems autonomously manage, invest, insure, and optimize a person's financial life with minimal human intervention. Users will set broad goals ("retire by 55", "buy a house in 3 years"), and AI will do the rest, working 24/7 behind the scenes.

4. AI-Powered Financial Crime Fighting

AI will become even more essential in detecting complex forms of financial fraud, cybercrime, and money laundering schemes. Machine learning models will increasingly

outsmart fraudsters, analyzing patterns humans would never spot.

Graph 1: Investment in AI Technologies by FinTech Companies (2015-2025, Projected)

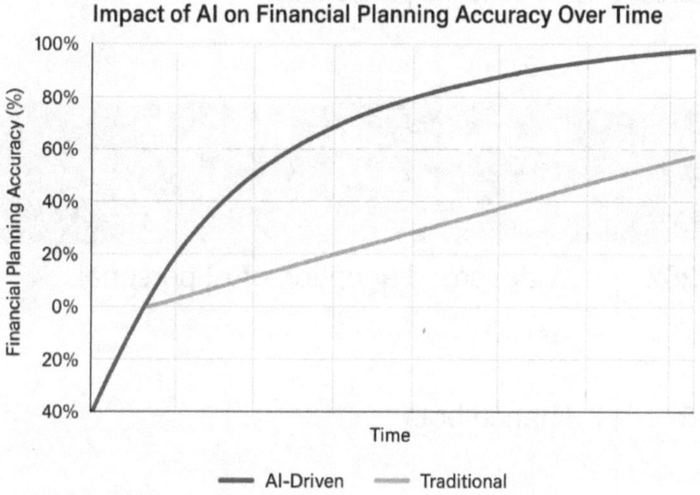

This graph shows the sharp rise in AI investment across FinTech firms, highlighting the accelerating belief in AI's transformative power.

Predictions for the Next Decade

The coming decade will bring profound changes, driven by both technological innovation and shifting consumer expectations.

Here are some concrete predictions:

Year	Predicted Development
2026	Widespread adoption of AI personal finance bots
2028	AI-led predictive banking becomes mainstream

2029	Introduction of fully autonomous robo-banks (no human staff)
2030	AI manages 50%+ of global assets under management (AUM)
2032	Decentralized AI financial ecosystems emerge (combining DeFi + AI)

How Businesses and Individuals Can Prepare for AI-Led Financial Innovation

For Businesses:

- **Invest in Talent and Training:** Companies must invest in AI literacy among employees and recruit data scientists and AI engineers.
- **Prioritize Ethical AI:** With regulators focusing more on bias and transparency, businesses must ensure their AI models are explainable, fair, and compliant.
- **Adapt Business Models:** Traditional banks and financial institutions need to pivot towards AI-driven models or risk becoming obsolete. Partnering with FinTech startups can accelerate transformation.

For Individuals:

- **Build Financial Data Literacy:** Understanding how AI algorithms work can help individuals make better financial decisions and protect themselves from biases or misjudgments made by automated systems.
- **Embrace Smart Tools:** From budgeting apps to robo-advisors, individuals should start using AI-powered tools to better manage personal finances.
- **Plan for Career Disruptions:** As AI automates many finance jobs, individuals must continuously upskill, focusing on roles that require human judgment, creativity, and emotional intelligence.

Table 2: Skills Needed for the AI-Driven Financial Future

Skill	Why It Matters
Data Analysis	To interpret AI outputs effectively
AI and Machine Learning Basics	To understand how financial AI works
Ethical Awareness	To ensure responsible AI deployment
Cybersecurity Knowledge	To protect personal and business assets

Emotional Intelligence	For roles requiring client interaction and trust

Graph 2: Projected Impact of AI on Financial Sector Employment (2015-2035)

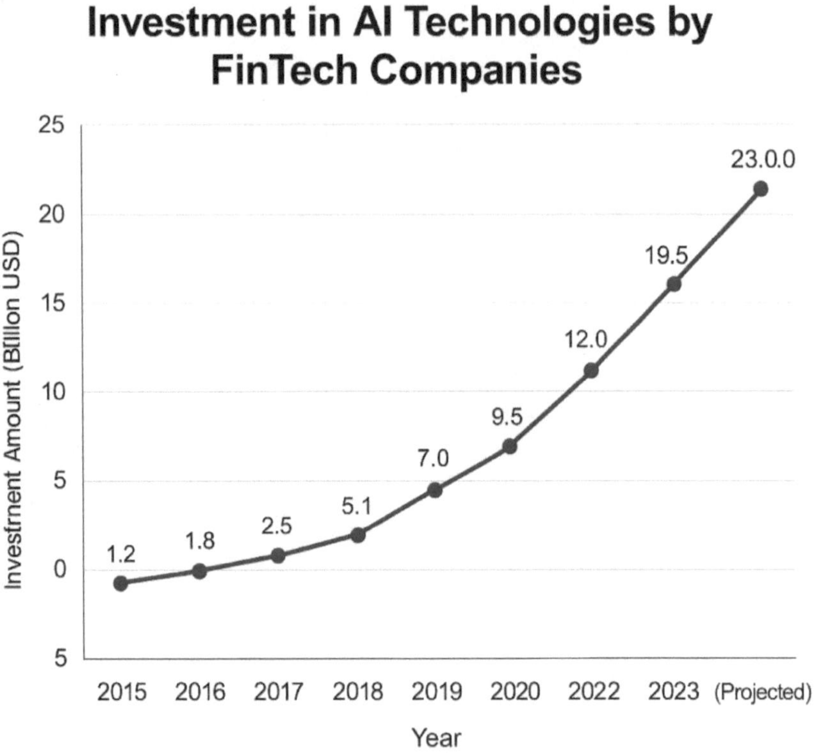

This graph illustrates how AI will affect various financial job sectors, showing both job reductions and new opportunity areas created by AI advancements.

Summary

The future of AI in FinTech is not a distant dream - it is unfolding right now. As AI becomes more autonomous, intelligent, and integrated into daily financial life, it will dramatically reshape everything from how we save and invest to how institutions manage risk and serve customers. Those who **embrace AI**, **adapt quickly**, and **cultivate the right skills** will thrive in this new financial era. The key will be to view AI not as a threat but as a powerful ally - one that can unlock a smarter, more inclusive, and more efficient financial future.

Conclusion: Charting a New Financial Future with AI

As we close this journey through the transformative power of the use cases of artificial intelligence in finance, one thing is clear: the future is being already built today.

AI is not just a tool - it is a partner, an advisor, and in many ways, a revolutionary force reshaping how we bank, invest, lend, and protect our assets. Whether through robo-advisors democratizing investment advice, AI-driven lending models offering financial inclusion, or decentralized systems reinventing trust, we are entering an era where finance becomes smarter, faster, and more human-centered.

However, with great power comes great responsibility. As leaders, innovators, and consumers, it is up to us to ensure

AI in finance remains ethical, transparent, and fair. Technology must serve humanity - not replace it.

The next decade will belong to those who adapt, who embrace innovation without losing sight of human values. Whether you are a business leader, a startup founder, an investor, or simply a curious mind, you have a role to play in this revolution.

The financial future is not something we must wait for. It is something we can create - today.

About the Author

Raijo Nirmal has spent his life at the intersection of logic and creativity. A finance expert who thinks like and is also an engineer, a strategist who speaks through music, and a CEO who still races motorcycles when he needs to remember what calculated risk really feels like He graduated with an MBA in International Business and an MS in Finance from UI Chicago and has completed his bachelors from Government Engineering College, Barton Hill, India with a focus in Electronics and Communication Engineering. Raijo approaches money like a scientist - dissecting systems, questioning assumptions, and rebuilding them smarter. This unique blend led him to launch Finnimo, an AI startup company that simplifies your personal finance management. This book grew from that mission. After years in the trenches of FinTech, he realized something unsettling: the finance world was completely in the race of AI, but no one was explaining what it *meant* for real lives. So he wrote the field manual he wished had existed.

Beyond spreadsheets and startups, Raijo is a classically trained pianist who has secured a distinction in Grade 8 level Piano Performance examinations from the London College of Music who still composes music and trains young talents. He is also a passionate photographer and you can always see him carry his camera wherever he goes. Apart from this he is also a trained professional motorcycle racer who is extremely passionate about cars and motorbikes. As a matter of fact, he has done a solo motorbike ride from Kanyakumari to Kashmir and Leh,

Ladakh (the entire span of India) on his motorbike which is just one of his many other trip in the country.

He truly believes finance should empower people, not confuse them - whether through smarter apps, clearer books, or just helping someone understand their own money story better. Currently based in Chicago ,Illinois, you can find him always on the move either through spreadsheets, musical keys or he might just be on another roadtrip.

Acknowledgments

Writing *The Thinking Dollar* has been one of the most humbling experiences of my life, not just because of the late nights and coffee-stained drafts, but because it reminded me how rarely any meaningful work is done alone. This book exists because of the people who believed in it even before it was an idea, who pushed me when I doubted myself, and who generously shared their wisdom along the way.

First to my mentor, Dr. Giby Raphael - You saw the potential in my half-formed thoughts long before I did. Thank you for the tough questions, the relentless curiosity, and for teaching me that the best ideas aren't found, they're forged. This book would still be scribbles in a notebook if not for your guidance.

To Lindstrom Elsa, my literary compass - You didn't just fix my commas, you challenged me to say what I meant, boldly and clearly. Your patience (and red pen) turned jargon into storytelling, and your honesty kept me from taking the easy way out. Every page is better because of you. Thank you.

To the FinTech rebels and AI pioneers whose work inspired this book: You're the reason I wake up optimistic about finance's future. My gratitude to my professors at my business school, you lit the spark. Those lectures in which it hit me, *"Money is just data with a story"* - that's where this all began.

To my friends, you were my sounding boards, my cheerleaders, and occasionally my therapists. Thanks for pretending to care about algorithmic bias over everything, for reading my terrible first drafts, and for never letting me forget that finance should serve people, not the other way around. To my family, your quiet faith in me was everything. Thanks for the 3 a.m. prep talks and for never asking, *"When will you be done?"* (even though you were thinking it) and to my partner for keeping me grounded and reminding me there's a world outside fintech.

Finally, to you, the reader: Thank you for trusting me with your time and attention. If this book helps you see money and the systems behind it a little differently, then every sleepless night was worth it.

With gratitude,

Raijo Nirmal

Made in United States
Troutdale, OR
05/14/2025

31296000R00100